CONTENTS

GETTING STARTED

About one billion people all over the world speak English. This book will help you talk to them!

This book will teach you 500 essential words and phrases to communicate in all kinds of everyday situations – from making friends, to shopping for clothes, or finding your way around!

The United Kingdom and Great Britain

The United Kingdom is England, Scotland, Wales and Northern Ireland.

Great Britain is England, Scotland and Wales.

People speak English in many countries, including:

The United Kingdom	Ireland	Jamaica
	South Africa	Nigeria
The United States of America	New Zealand	Zimbabwe
		Kenya
Canada	India	
		Sudan
Australia	Pakistan	
		Zambia

UK FACTS

- About 60.5 million people live in the United Kingdom.

- British money is the pound (£).

- Be careful when you cross the road in the UK! People drive on the left hand side of the road.

- The most famous writer in the world was from the UK. His name was William Shakespeare.

KEY WORDS

Yes.	Of course!	Excuse me.
No.	I don't know.	Please...
Maybe.	Sorry!	Thank you.

HELP!

If you don't understand what an English-speaking person is saying to you, here are some useful phrases:

I don't understand.

Please speak more slowly.

How do you say...?

Could you repeat that, please?

Go for it! Have fun! Good luck!

MAKING NEW FRIENDS

Hello!   Hi!

What's your name?

My name's Anna.

What languages do you speak?

I speak English and French.

Where are you from?

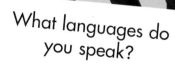

Spain
(Spanish)

Italy
(Italian)

Poland
(Polish)

I'm from Britain.
(I'm British.)

France
(French)

Germany
(German)

China
(Chinese)

I have
a boyfriend/
a girlfriend.

Can you give me
your mobile
number?

Do you want to dance
with me?

What are you into?

fashion

dancing

sport

films

video games

Can you give me your
email address?

My email is...

Good bye!

See you
soon!

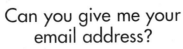

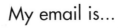

DATES AND TIMES

How old are you?

I'm sixteen years old.

When's your birthday?

My birthday's on the 11th of May.

How many?

1	2	3	4	5	6	7	8	9	10	11
one	two	three	four	five	six	seven	eight	nine	ten	eleven

12	13	14	15	16	17	18	19	20
twelve	thirteen	fourteen	fifteen	sixteen	seventeen	eighteen	nineteen	twenty

What's the time?

quarter past six

ten past four

half past ten

twenty to two

quarter to twelve

one o'clock

Days of the week

See you at seven o'clock on Friday evening!

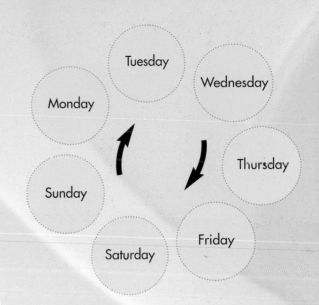

Monday
Tuesday
Wednesday
Thursday
Friday
Saturday
Sunday

The year

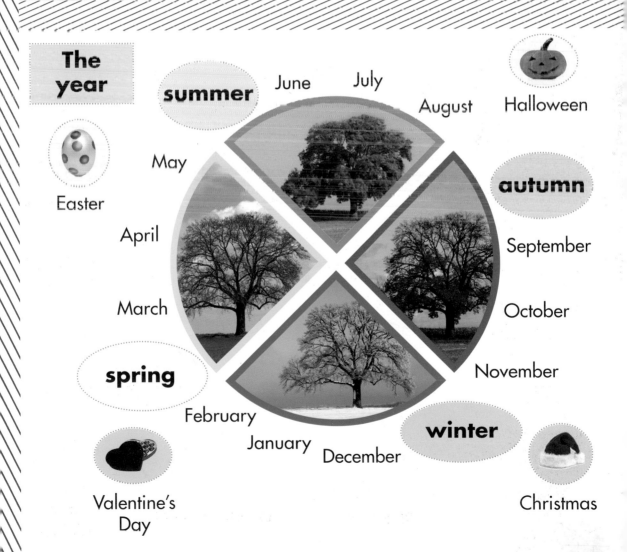

summer

June
July
August
Halloween

autumn

May
Easter

April

March

September

October

November

spring

February
January
December

winter

Valentine's Day

Christmas

FOOD AND DRINK

What would you like?

My favourite meal is hamburger and milkshake.

Menu

ham

chips

chicken

pasta

bread

a sandwich

green vegetables

a mixed salad

a pizza

soup

I hate fruit!

I drink milk in the morning.

I eat salad every day.

Drinks

an orange juice

a glass of water

a hot chocolate

a fizzy drink

Ice cream

What flavours have you got?

coffee

vanilla

strawberry

chocolate

lemon

mint

WHO'S WHO?

1 She's got blonde hair.

4 blue eyes

2 pierced ears

5 straight hair

3 long hair

6 glasses

7 a fringe

9 teeth

8 mouth

10 braces

11 nose

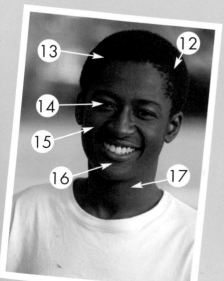

12 He's got black hair.

15 cheek

13 short hair

16 chin

14 brown eyes

17 neck

Here's my family.

Have you got any brothers and sisters?

I've got two brothers and a sister.

my dad

my mum

my brother

my sister

me

my grandmother

my grandfather

my cousin

my aunt

my uncle

Pets

Have you got any pets?

I've got a dog.

a mouse

a hamster

a budgie

a cat

a goldfish

a rabbit

a snake

FASHION

My favourite clothes are jeans and t-shirts.

Can I try this on?

Does it suit me?

Yes, it looks great!

I wear trainers at the weekend.

| blue | green | yellow | orange | red | pink | purple | black | white |

earrings

a skirt

a cap

a hooded top

a scarf

sunglasses

a jacket

gloves

a dress

a bag

a belt

shorts

sandals

a pullover

trousers

shoes

TECHNOLOGY

I'll send a text message.

I chat with my friends
on the Internet.

Shall we take a photo?

I need to check my emails.

Don't forget to charge
your mobile!

We love video games.

a radio

a camcorder

a laptop

A computer

a computer screen

a webcam

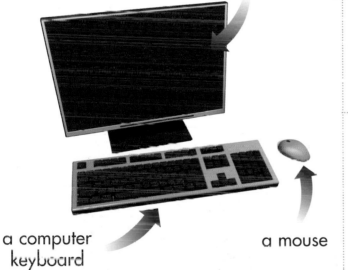
a computer
keyboard

a mouse

a camera

a games console

an ipod/mp3 player

a DVD player

a mobile phone

a DVD

a television

FREE TIME

I play in a band.

I like hip-hop.	dance	rock
heavy metal	R 'n' B	pop

Do you play an instrument?

keyboard

piano

violin

drums

electric guitar

saxophone

flute

Which football team do you support?

We lost the match 1–0.

We won the last match.

What sport do you like?

rugby

tennis

horse-riding

swimming

cycling

running

judo

skiing

rock climbing

IN TOWN

This is my house.

I live in a block of flats.

a zoo

an Internet cafe

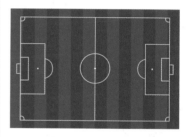

a football pitch

a sports centre

a swimming pool

a library

a hotel

a restaurant

a hairdresser's salon

Is there a coffee shop near here?

The theme park is brilliant!

a police station

a museum

a post office

a park

a cinema

a campsite

toilets

a tourist information office

a hospital

SHOPPING

I love shopping with my friends!

How much does this cost?

Twenty pounds, please.

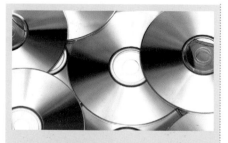

a music shop

a game store

a clothes shop

a gift shop

a sports shop

a cake shop

a shoe shop

a supermarket

I'd like two postcards, please.

Oh no! It's too expensive!

a CD

stamps

an umbrella

batteries

sweets

lip gloss

a magazine

perfume

open

closed

entrance

exit

AT SCHOOL

I'm very good at maths.

I'm terrible at art.

I have a lot of homework!

I walk to school.

I take the bus.

School subjects

French

Spanish

Geography

History

Science

I.C.T.

Drama

Technology

P.E.

Inside the classroom

teacher   a board

a desk

students

a chair

School starts at 8:45.

School finishes at 3:30.

In my school bag

pens

pencils

a pencil case

an eraser

an exercise book

a memory stick

a dictionary

a calculator

TRAVEL

We usually get the bus to go to town.

Two singles to the town centre, please.

a plane

a boat/ferry

a motorbike

a taxi

an airport

a train

a car

a bus

a scooter

a bus stop

a railway station

Can you tell
me how
to get to the
station, please?

Carry on down
this road.

What time is the next train to...?

Which platform is it?

Turn right.

Turn left.

Go straight
on.

at the
roundabout

at the
crossroads

at the traffic
lights

at the
bridge

How do I get to the beach?

Take bus 23.

JOBS

I'd like to be a doctor.

a sportsperson

a dentist

a vet

a journalist

When I leave school,
I'm going to work
in a shop.

an office

outdoors

a factory

a chef

mechanic

a photographer

a firefighter

a scientist

a police officer

I have a part-time job.

babysitting

walking dogs

mowing the lawn

I deliver newspapers in the morning.

HOW DO YOU FEEL?

How are you?

 Not so great.

 I'm fine, thanks.

I'm happy.

I'm sad.

I'm scared.

I'm a bit bored.

I'm having fun here.

I'm angry.

What do you think?

It's really cool!

great

rubbish

easy

fun

difficult

interesting

Not feeling well?

I have toothache.

I'm hungry.

I'm thirsty.

I feel sick.

I'm cold.

I've got a temperature.

I'd like to see a doctor.

I'm hot.

I'm tired.

I feel sleepy.

I've got a stomach ache.

I've got a headache.

TOP TIPS

ENGLISH VERBS

TO BE

I am	I'm not
You are	You're not
He/she/it is	He/she/it isn't
We are	We aren't
They are	They aren't

TO HAVE

I have	I don't have
You have	You don't have
He/she has	He/she doesn't have
We have	We don't have
They have	They don't have

TO LIKE

I like	I don't like
You like	You don't like
He/she likes	He/she doesn't like
We like	We don't like
They like	They don't like

TO BE ABLE TO

I can	I can't
You can	You can't
He/she/it can	He/she/it can't
We can	We can't
They can	They can't

TO DO

I do	I don't
You do	You don't
He/she/it does	He/she/it doesn't
We do	We don't
They do	They don't

UK MEASUREMENTS

1 inch = 2.54 centimetres

1 foot = 0.3 metres

1 mile = 1.6 kilometres

1 stone = 6.35 kilograms

UK AND US ENGLISH

UK	US
toilet	restroom
shop	store
football	soccer
mobile phone	cell phone

UK	US
trousers	pants
chips	french fries
autumn	fall
block of flats	apartment block